High-Interest Activities

for enrichment and extension

in Vocabulary

Written by Gunter Schymkiw

Illustrated by Louise Williams

Published by Prim-Ed Publishing

Foreword

The activities in these books will stimulate children's interest in language and vocabulary and will encourage further reading and writing activities.

This book specialises in vocabulary; it covers vocabulary building, rhyming, classifying, syllables and multiple meanings.

Contents

Interesting Words - Fact Sheet

English is a language made up of many words borrowed from other languages.

It is interesting to trace the origins of some of our words. If something is **trivial** it is of little importance. The word comes from the language of Ancient Rome, Latin. It means 'three roads'. The junction of three roads was the place where weary travellers often stopped to chat idly to relieve the boredom of travel.

To **meander** is to wander aimlessly. This word comes to us from the Greek word **Maiandros**, the name of a winding river in Turkey.

Geometry is the study of shapes. It comes from the Ancient Greek word **geometrein** which means 'to measure the land'.

Kindergarten comes from two German words, meaning 'children's garden'.

Soccer is the most popular football code. Its official name was 'Association Football'. The term soccer came into popular use as an extended form of the 'soc' in 'association'.

The **Solar System** takes its name from Sol, the Roman God of the Sun.

In politics a **gerrymander** is when an electorate boundary is arranged to favour a political party or candidate.

This word comes from the USA where governor Gerry from the state of Massachusetts arranged an electorate in the shape of a salamander so it would include people likely to favour someone he wanted elected.

'Gerry' comes from his name, and 'mander' from salamander.

It would be a bit like having a vote for class captain but only allowing your friends to vote.

*Gerry's electorate.

The people in the white houses are Gerry's supporters.

The people in the black houses support Gerry's opposition.

Divers who need to stay under water for extended periods of time use **SCUBA diving equipment.** This equipment, which includes tanks of compressed air, gets its name from the initials of the words 'Self-contained Underwater Breathing Apparatus'.

Foolscap size paper is so called because it once had the watermark of the dunce's cap imprinted on it.

The dunce's cap was a nasty tradition. Children who were unable to do some work at school were made to wear this hat to show they were 'foolish'.

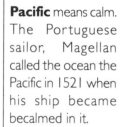

Pacific means calm. The Portuguese sailor, Magellan called the ocean the Pacific in 1521 when his ship became becalmed in it.

Butterflies are so called because it was once believed that they stole milk and butter.

The **sperm whale** is so called because of the oil in its head. The whale's head contains about 2 000 litres of this oil which was used for many years in machinery. Early sailors thought the oil was the whale's sperm.

The word **tomato** comes to us from the Aztec people of Mexico. They were the first people to grow this fruit.

Telephone comes from two Greek words. 'Tele' means 'far off' and 'Phone' means 'a sound'.

Find the origins of these words:
RADAR
SONAR

Do a project on some interesting words.

See how many words you can find beginning with tri-, quad- and cent-.

A. *Next to each word, write the language or country from where it originates.*

1. trivial _____
2. geometry _____
3. telephone _____
4. kindergarten _____

5. meander _____
6. tomato _____
7. solar system _____
8. gerrymander _____

B. *Answer in complete sentences.*

1. Which people of ancient times spoke the language called Latin? _____
   _____

2. Why are butterflies so called? _____
   _____

3. Why was the Pacific Ocean so called? _____
   _____

4. What does the acronym SCUBA stand for? _____
   _____

C. *Use a dictionary to find three words beginning with:*

1. T E L E _____
2. T R I _____
3. Q U A D _____
4. C E N T _____

D. *Find words with these meanings on the sheet.*

1. Where things join ____ ____ ____ ____ t ____ ____ ____
2. From Portugal ____ ____ ____ ____ ____ g ____ ____ ____ ____
3. Mexican Indians ____ ____ ____ ____ c ____
4. A border ____ ____ ____ n ____ ____ ____ ____
5. A member of the amphibian family
   ____ ____ ____ ____ ____ ____ ____ ____ ____ r

E. *Draw, label and colour two words written about on the Facts Sheet.*
   Colour all the pictures on the Facts Sheet.

Add-a-Word

Add a word meaning 'something worn on the head' to the letter 'c' and you get a word that means 'talk': C + HAT = 'chat'

Do these the same way as the example:

1. B + not out = where we put rubbish ____ ____ ____

2. B + you and I = a form of transport ____ ____ ____

3. T + a common domesticated bird = not now ____ ____ ____ ____

4. S + a baby's bed = a person from Scotland ____ ____ ____ ____

5. P + a beam of sunlight = what you might do in church ____ ____ ____ ____

6. G + sick = what a fish uses to breathe ____ ____ ____ ____

7. H + as well as = part of the body ____ ____ ____ ____

8. F + a common colour = a boy's name ____ ____ ____ ____

9. B + a number = what dogs like ____ ____ ____ ____

10. S + not high = a snail's pace ____ ____ ____ ____

11. F + part of the body = where wheat is grown ____ ____ ____ ____

12. S + a small fairy-like being = you ____ ____ ____ ____

13. B + Noah's boat = the skin of a tree ____ ____ ____ ____

14. D + to tear = what a leaky tap does ____ ____ ____ ____

15. H + a long thin fish = part of the foot ____ ____ ____ ____

16. P + writing fluid = a colour ____ ____ ____ ____

17. S + a step = where rockets fly ____ ____ ____ ____

18. P + biting insects = trousers ____ ____ ____ ____

19. T + water from the sky = form of transport ____ ____ ____ ____

20. C + what's on top of your head = piece of furniture ____ ____ ____ ____ ____

21. ST + something worn on the finger = something used to tie parcels

    ____ ____ ____ ____ ____ ____

22. C + the sound made by bees = a friend ____ ____ ____ ____

23. B + to hurry = something you use on your hair ____ ____ ____ ____ ____

24. SP + something shot from a bow = a bird ____ ____ ____ ____ ____

25. D + a large flow of water = the person at the front of a bus

    ____ ____ ____ ____ ____ ____

26. CL + the middle traffic light = to climb ____ ____ ____ ____ ____ ____

27. TH + below = storm noise ____ ____ ____ ____ ____

28. T + what a camel has = to hit ____ ____ ____ ____

29. S + part of the mouth = cricket fielding position ____ ____ ____ ____ ____

30. S + what birds have = sways ____ ____ ____ ____ ____

Our Colourful Language

The words related to the topic can be found in blocks in the puzzle. Words read letter to letter in any direction <u>except diagonally</u>. Every letter has been used. No letter is shared by words. One example is done for you. *Colour the answer blocks that connect one another in different colours.*

G	B	L	A	C	Y	E	R	G	T	B	E
R	E	E	N	K	M	W	H	O	U	L	U
Y	E	L	W	C	A	T	I	K	I	A	R
P	U	L	I	A	Y	T	T	C	N	N	O
R	R	O	T	T	V	E	E	A	T	G	K
E	P	W	H	E	N	R	D	L	H	E	N
D	L	S	**G**	B	L	A	W	B	E	P	I
C	E	T	**R**	**E**	A	R	F	P	A	T	R
R	H	R	**E**	C	G	B	E	E	D	A	
E	E	K	**N**	K	R	L	U	R	L	L	
S	A	R	T	E	D	E	E	E	C	O	E
C	E	N	T	A	T	H	N	H	O	U	S

BLUE COLLAR
BLACK DEATH
WHITE DWARF
PURPLE HEART
IN THE PINK
BLACK OUT
BLACKCAT
REDTAPE
ORANGE
BLUE
<u>GREEN</u>
GREEN WITH ENVY
YELLOW STREAK
RED CRESCENT
GREEN HOUSE
GREY MATTER

Use words from the list to fill these gaps.

1. To be sad is to be_____.

2. In Muslim countries, the Red Cross is called the _____.

3. Political _____ is often the cause of delays in making amendments to policies.

4. Delicate plants are grown in a _____.

5. Someone who is a coward is said to have a _____.

6. Many people are superstitious. Many believe the number 13, walking under ladders, breaking a mirror and a _____ walking past you can bring bad luck.

7. A _____ worker is one who works in industry.

8. Tangerine, satsuma, mandarin and clementine are a type of _____.

9. Someone who has an ability to grow plants is said to have _____ fingers.

10. To be jealous is to be _____.

11. To be in good health is to be _____.

12. The brain is sometimes referred to as the _____.

13. The bubonic plague that swept through Europe and Asia during the 14th century killing 50 million people was called the _____.

14. A member of the US armed forces wounded in action is awarded a medal called the _____.

15. Just before a star dies, it shrinks and increases in density to become what is known as a _____.

16. In time of war a _____ was when many of the lights of a city were turned off to conserve electricity and confuse enemy aircraft.

Find the meanings of: Black Maria, Blackguard, Blueprint, White Goods, Greenhorn.

The words related to the topic can be found in blocks in the puzzle. Words read letter to letter in any direction <u>except diagonally</u>. Every letter has been used. No letter is shared by words. One example is done. *Colour answer blocks that connect one another different colours.*

U	T	A	K	N	O	R	T	H	N	O	R
T	U	C	C	J	T	M	B	O	N	E	T
N	B	K	A	U	U	U	C	N	B	D	H
A	E	R	I	B	M	T	H	O	O	A	B
C	A	B	B	J	U	B	O	O	N	P	N
N	Y	O	E	R	Y	O	G	C	H	O	E
A	E	O	O	I	T	Y	A	P	O	M	D
C	A	B	O	E	O	O	G	O	O	P	A
O	Y	E	G	E	M	T	A	P	M	O	B
G	O	**N**	E	W	T	A	R	T	A	R	E
T	G	**I**	E	A	O	M	T	S	E	T	S
I	**N**	**T**	G	G	G	A	W	A	G	G	A

TIN TIN   GO-GO
CANCAN   TUTU
BERI-BERI   AYE AYE
BOO-BOO   ACK-ACK
GEE-GEE   JUB JUB
TUM TUM   YOYO
TOM-TOM   TARTAR
TSE TSE   POMPOM
BONBON   PAGO PAGO
CHOO CHOO
WAGGA WAGGA
NORTH-NORTH
BADEN BADEN

Choose from the double words in the list to fill the gaps below. Clues are given in brackets.

1. <u>T I N T I N</u> (a comic strip character) has a dog called Snowy.
2. Have you seen any _____ (bird in the poem 'Jabberwocky') birds flying about lately?
3. There is a nest in the _____ (tree in the poem 'Jabberwocky') tree in Jim's backyard.
4. _____ is a city in Germany's Black Forest region famous for its hot springs.
5. The _____ fly lives in Africa and spreads many deadly diseases.
6. Gary was a good boy so his mother gave him a (sweet) _____.
7. Peter comes from (city in NSW, Australia) _____.
8. 'I've made a big (mistake) _____,' said the Prime Minister.
9. '(Yes) _____ Captain,' said the sailor, saluting.
10. I wept uncontrollably when the string on my (toy) _____ broke.
11. The cowboy rode into the sunset on his (horse) _____.
12. American Indians often sent messages with a (drum) _____.
13. _____-west is a direction.
14. 'I must hurry or I'll miss my (train) _____,' said the businessman.
15. Colin thought he had _____ (disease caused by a thiamine deficiency), but it was just a cold.
16. The ballerina wore a white (ballet dress) _____.
17. 'I want to be either a _____ dancer or _____ dancer when I grow up,' said Lisa.
18. A _____ was an anti-aircraft gun used to shoot the enemy planes during World War II. Fire from the gun was known as _____.
19. A spiteful woman is sometimes called a _____.
20. _____ is a port on an island in the Pacific Ocean.

Double Trouble

Change the double letter in each word to form a new word or words. *Write the word on the line provided and then match it to its meaning on the right-hand side. Use different colours when matching words with meanings.*

Word		New word	Meaning
slipper	=	_____	light horse-drawn cart
stammer	=	S T A G G E R	clever
Russian	=	_____	jumped
baggier	=	_____	scoundrel
skimmed	=	_____	walk with difficulty
skimmed	=	_____	fight
skimmed	=	_____	something that gets in the way
babble	=	_____	slipped
babble	=	_____	dispenser of Easter eggs
bully	=	_____	thinner
bully	=	_____	confuse

Word		New word	Meaning
sullen	=	_____	lottery
puddle	=	_____	without warning
supper	=	_____	sewing tool
supper	=	_____	crossword
rattle	=	_____	a thousand lots of a thousand
bitter	=	_____	be in pain
bitter	=	_____	more choosy
mission	=	_____	more humorous
furrier	=	_____	a season
furrier	=	_____	larger
noodle	=	_____	person who tries to buy something at an auction

Word		New word	Meaning
dazzle	=	_____	thing that directs a ship
dazzle	=	_____	mottled colour horse's coat
pussy	=	_____	slang word for rugby
pussy	=	_____	young dog
pussy	=	_____	eraser
stood	=	_____	horse
buffet	=	_____	damp
wattle	=	_____	swollen
wattle	=	_____	paste used to fix glass into windowpanes
sorry	=	_____	shot from a gun
runner	=	_____	ducks do this in water
runner	=	_____	how ducks walk
runner	=	_____	type of pancake

A Horse Vocabulary

The following words all relate to horses. Use these to complete the sentences below. Each word is used once. Colour the answer boxes as you find the answers.

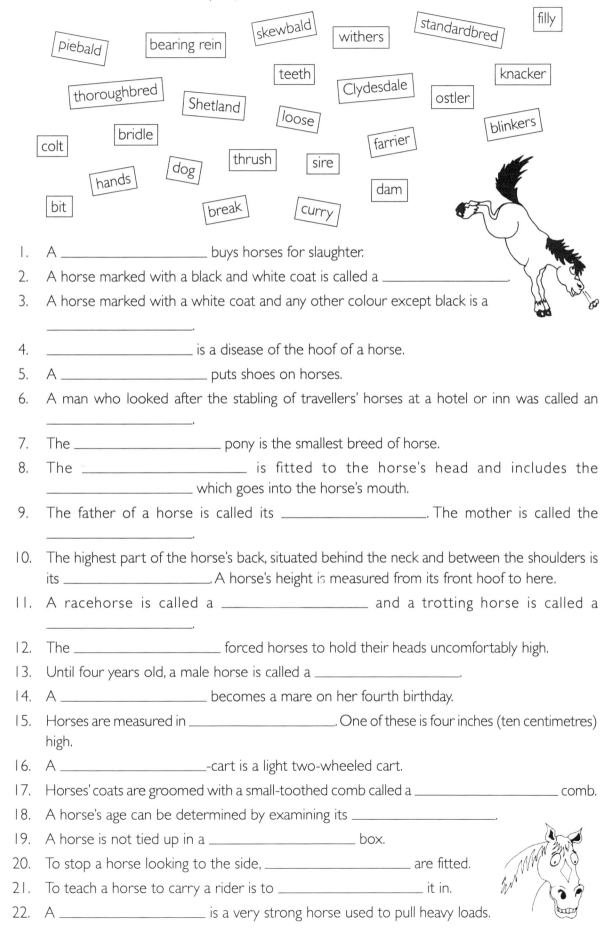

skewbald withers standardbred filly

piebald bearing rein

teeth knacker

Clydesdale ostler

thoroughbred Shetland loose

blinkers

bridle farrier

colt thrush sire

dog dam

hands

bit break curry

1. A _____ buys horses for slaughter.

2. A horse marked with a black and white coat is called a _____.

3. A horse marked with a white coat and any other colour except black is a
    _____.

4. _____ is a disease of the hoof of a horse.

5. A _____ puts shoes on horses.

6. A man who looked after the stabling of travellers' horses at a hotel or inn was called an
    _____.

7. The _____ pony is the smallest breed of horse.

8. The _____ is fitted to the horse's head and includes the
    _____ which goes into the horse's mouth.

9. The father of a horse is called its _____. The mother is called the
    _____.

10. The highest part of the horse's back, situated behind the neck and between the shoulders is
    its _____. A horse's height is measured from its front hoof to here.

11. A racehorse is called a _____ and a trotting horse is called a
    _____.

12. The _____ forced horses to hold their heads uncomfortably high.

13. Until four years old, a male horse is called a _____.

14. A _____ becomes a mare on her fourth birthday.

15. Horses are measured in _____. One of these is four inches (ten centimetres)
    high.

16. A _____-cart is a light two-wheeled cart.

17. Horses' coats are groomed with a small-toothed comb called a _____ comb.

18. A horse's age can be determined by examining its _____.

19. A horse is not tied up in a _____ box.

20. To stop a horse looking to the side, _____ are fitted.

21. To teach a horse to carry a rider is to _____ it in.

22. A _____ is a very strong horse used to pull heavy loads.

Places Where People and Animals Live

The words related to the topic can be found in blocks in the puzzle. Words read letter to letter in any direction except diagonally. Every letter has been used. No letter is shared by words. One example is done for you. *Colour answer blocks that connect one another different colours.*

E	Y	R	I	F	**C**	**L**	D	O	K	E	N
S	K	C	E	O	**E**	**L**	G	V	M	O	N
B	A	A	M	R	M	N	U	E	A	N	E
S	R	R	A	C	O	Y	E	C	S	T	L
E	S	S	N	V	N	A	L	O	S	E	R
O	U	E	N	E	N	H	B	T	H	L	Y
H	G	V	A	I	T	S	A	E	E	L	P
E	N	A	R	G	L	S	T	S	C	O	O
V	O	C	A	O	O	E	R	T	R	O	F
I	L	A	H	W	S	E	S	U	O	H	K
H	E	R	N	E	R	W	O	N	W	E	R
L	O	D	G	E	R	A	R	A	M	B	O
											W

WORKHOUSES   LODGE
MANOR   DOVECOTE
KENNEL   COOP
HIVE   STABLE
MONASTERY   FORM
FORTRESS   GUNYAH
LONGHOUSES   EYRIE
BARRACKS   WHARE
CONVENT   MANSE
SHELL   WEB
CARAVAN
IGLOO
CELL
WARREN

1. A horse is kept in a _____.
2. A mole's underground home is called a _____.
3. The connecting tunnels of a rabbit colony are called a _____.
4. An eagle builds its _____ high up on a mountain ledge.
5. A colony of bees lives in a _____.
6. People often build a _____ for dogs.
7. A hare lives in a hollow of thick grass known as a _____.
8. A beaver's home is called a _____.
9. A spider spins a _____ for its home.
10. A snail's home is its _____.
11. A structure people build to keep doves is a _____.
12. Chickens are kept in a _____.
13. Soldiers are housed in _____.
14. The _____ was the traditional home of New Zealand's Maoris.
15. The Dyak people of Borneo live in _____.
16. The traditional Inuit person's (Eskimo's) home is the _____.
17. In the 19th century, poor people were given accommodation in _____ in return for unpaid work.
18. The _____ is the traditional home of the gypsy.
19. Monks live in a _____.
20. A lord lives in _____.
21. Nuns live in a _____.
22. A prisoner lives in a ___CELL___.
23. An Australian Aboriginal shelter is a _____.
24. A minister of religion lives in a _____.

Words and Expressions from Other Languages

The words related to the topic can be found in blocks in the puzzle. Words read letter to letter in any direction except diagonally. Every letter has been used. No letter is shared by words. One example is done for you. *Colour answer blocks that connect one another different colours.*

A	R	D	N	O	P	A	U	T	A	T	S
M	D	E	X	O	E	N	S	H	C	A	D
G	I	Z	P	V	R	N	Q	S	H	T	Z
R	A	S	O	O	D	O	U	O	U	I	E
A	S	I	P	M	I	N	I	D	N	N	L
L	V	L	U	L	I	E	M	T	D	H	A
A	O	E	D	E	C	O	A	S	E	C	I
M	U	A	U	I	T	L	D	U	I	S	T
O	S	P	L	A	G	O	E	L	G	R	A
D	E	M	E	T	N	E	R	R	E	D	N
S	U	P	T	E	N	O	T	B	R	H	A
F	U	G	I	R	I	N	G	O	A	G	W

REPONDEZ S'IL VOUS PLAIT
EAU DE COLOGNE
TEMPUS FUGIT
ERIN GO BRAGH
ANNO DOMINI
WANDERLUST
<u>MARDI GRAS</u>
STATUS QUO
VOX POPULI
NOTRE DAME
DEI GRATIA
SCHNITZEL
DACHSHUND
A LA MODE

It is not uncommon for languages to borrow expressions from other languages. The French, for example, have made the term 'le weekend' part of their language. *Match the words and expressions in the list with their English equivalents below.*

1. _____ means Shrove Tuesday, which is commonly called Pancake Day. (French)

2. _____ means 'time flies'.

3. A _____ is a cutlet. (German)

4. _____ means 'Our Lady' and is a name given to churches dedicated to the Virgin Mary, mother of Christ. (French)

5. _____ means 'long live Ireland'. (Irish)

6. _____ is the desire to travel. (German)

7. _____ is a perfume which literally means 'water of Cologne'. (French) (Cologne is a city in Germany.)

8. _____ means 'public opinion'. (Latin)

9. _____ means 'in the year of our Lord'. (Latin)

10. _____ means 'by the grace of God'. (Latin)

11. A _____ is a dog whose name means 'badger dog'. (German)

12. If something is _____ it is in fashion. (French)

13. The _____ is the existing state of affairs. (Latin)

14. _____, often just written as initials, means 'please reply'. (French)

Which ancient people spoke the now dead language, Latin? _____

_____

_____

One Word to Describe a Group

Write one or two words to describe each of the groups below.

1. pine, willow, oak _____
2. plague, rabies, leprosy _____
3. cobra, taipan, python _____
4. *Times, Sun, Daily Telegraph* _____
5. trout, beam, whiting _____
6. veal, pork, beef _____
7. north, south, west _____
8. Beatles, Rolling Stones, INXS, 10CC _____
9. slipper, sandal, boot _____
10. Everton, Arsenal, Wolves _____
11. Carbine, Winchester, Colt _____
12. Shakespeare, Dahl, Dickens _____
13. dollar, pound, yen _____
14. Hobbs, Botham, Gower _____
15. black widow, trapdoor, funnelweb _____
16. Ford, ICI, Lloyds _____
17. Atlantic, Pacific, Indian _____
18. *Titanic, Lusitania, Endeavour* _____
19. kayak, raft, canoe _____
20. Islam, Christianity, Hinduism _____
21. two, four, six, eight _____
22. Datsun, Ford, BMW _____
23. ant, flea, fly _____
24. Spitfire, Cessna, Concorde _____
25. dictionary, atlas, encyclopaedia _____
26. rib, skull, spine _____
27. Clydesdale, Shetland thoroughbred _____
28. hammer, screwdriver, saw _____
29. Afghan, poodle, labrador _____
30. Thames, Humber, Mersey _____
31. Baltic, Irish, Mediterranean _____
32. ruby, diamond, sapphire _____
33. iron, lead, silver _____
34. daisy, tulip, rose _____
35. plum, cherry, peach _____
36. molar, canine, incisor _____
37. dromedary, bactrian _____
38. Simpson, Kalahari, Sahara _____
39. wood, iron, putter _____
40. Drake, Raleigh, Cook _____
41. one, three, five, seven _____
42. silk, cotton, linen _____
43. billy, nanny, kid _____
44. chips, pizza, hamburgers _____
45. dodo, ostrich, kiwi _____
46. Trafalgar, Piccadilly, Leicester _____
47. Czar, Kaiser, Emperor _____
48. offside, penalty, throw-in _____
49. Union Jack, Jolly Roger, Star-Spangled Banner _____
50. soccer, Australian Rules, rugby league _____
51. Van Gogh, Picasso _____
52. Sol, Betelgeuse, Alpha Centauri _____
53. guitar, violin, trumpet _____
54. flood, forest fire, earthquake _____
55. Thatcher, Major, Churchill _____
56. Robert the Bruce, Wallace, Rob Roy _____
57. *Flying Scotsman, Orient Express, Spirit of Progress* _____
58. Red Rum, Shergar, Nijinsky _____
59. Hercule Poirot, Charlie Chan, Sherlock Holmes _____
60. minim, crotchet, quaver _____
61. IBM, Apple, Sega _____
62. lettuce, cucumber, tomato _____
63. rock 'n' roll, jazz, classical _____
64. watercolour, oil, acrylic _____
65. Arabic, Roman, Greek _____

Animal Families - Fact Sheet

There are well over a million different types of animals living on the earth.

To make the study of animals easier, scientists have developed a system of grouping them according to their similar characteristics. This is called **Classification.**

Any animals with backbones are called **vertebrates.** Belonging to this group are birds, amphibians, reptiles, fish and mammals.

Fish live in water. They breathe oxygen from the water using gills. To move they use fins. They have a hard skin and a covering of scales to protect their bodies from the water.
The fishes' bodies are the same temperature as their surroundings. We say such animals are **cold-blooded.**

Amphibians, like fish, are cold-blooded animals. They both reproduce by means of eggs laid in water.

A seahorse is an unusual fish.

Reptiles are animals like snakes, lizards and crocodiles. Their skin is dry and scaly. Most lay eggs but some bear their young alive. They have lungs to breathe with and they are cold-blooded.

Amphibians are animals like frogs, toads and salamanders.
At different stages in their lives, they live in water and on land.
When they are young they live in water and breathe with gills. As adults they live on land, and they breathe with lungs and through their skin. Their skin is smooth and wet.

Birds' bodies are designed for flight. They have wings, feathers and light hollow bones.

Some birds, like the kiwi, emu, ostrich and penguin, can not fly.

Birds help us by controlling insect numbers. In China in the 1950s there was a campaign to eradicate sparrows.
When many of the birds were killed, insect numbers grew to plague proportions, so the campaign was stopped.

The dinosaurs were reptiles.

They are warm-blooded and breathe with lungs. Their young hatch from eggs.

Mammals are animals like goats, cats, dogs, elephants, and humans. They are warm-blooded. Their bodies have fur on them. Baby mammals are born from their mother and feed on the milk from her body.

The bat is a mammal that flies.

The echidna and platypus are unusual mammals as they lay eggs.
They belong to a special mammal group called **monotremes.**

The pouched **marsupials,** like the kangaroo, are members of a special group of mammals.

Animals without backbones are called **invertebrates.**
The largest family of this group is the **insect** family. Their bodies have three sections called the head, thorax and abdomen.
They have six legs and at some stage of their lives most have wings. Their skeletons are on the outside of their bodies. Such skeletons are called **exoskeletons.**
Most undergo several changes in their lives going from egg to larva to pupa to adult.

Some mammals, like whales and dolphins, live in water.

You are a mammal.

There are many other animal families. Find out what you can about them.

Do a project on some animals that you find interesting.

Animal Families - Worksheet

A. Answer in the sentences below in one or two words.

1. What is grouping similiar animals into families called? _____

2. What are animals with backbones called? _____

3. What do fish breathe with? _____

4. What do we call animals whose body temperature is the same as their surroundings?

    _____

5. Where do amphibians live when they are young? _____

6. What is the skin of a reptile like? _____

7. To which animal family did the dinosaurs belong? _____

8. What are birds' bones like? _____

9. To which mammal family do echidnas belong? _____

10. What is the largest family of the invertebrates? _____

B. List things that belong to the groups below. (You may need to research some answers.)

1. Three fish _____

2. Three amphibians _____

3. Three reptiles _____

4. Three flightless birds _____

5. Three mammals _____

6. Three body sections of an insect _____

7. Two stages in the life cycle of an insect _____

C. Answer the questions below in full sentences.

1. What is the skin of an amphibian like? _____

    _____

    _____

2. What is unusual about the skeleton of an insect? _____

    _____

    _____

3. If some nasty person called you an 'insect', give some reasons you could give them to

    let them know you are not. _____

    _____

    _____

    _____

Living Things

Add one letter to the beginning and end of these to make a word in the category.

Fish

1. ___ har ___
2. ___ hitin ___
3. ___ o ___
4. ___ laic ___
5. ___ erc ___
6. ___ rea ___
7. ___ almo ___
8. ___ ol ___
9. ___ ar ___
10. ___ rou ___
11. ___ ulle ___
12. ___ ackere ___
13. ___ un ___
14. ___ tingra ___
15. ___ lathea ___
16. ___ arli ___
17. ___ addoc ___
18. ___ arracud ___
19. ___ rope ___
20. ___ ik ___
21. ___ kat ___
22. ___ lounde ___

Reptiles

1. ___ s ___
2. ___ rass snak ___
3. ___ inosau ___
4. ___ ipe ___
5. ___ eck ___
6. ___ nacond ___
7. ___ attlesnak ___
8. ___ rocodil ___
9. ___ dde ___
10. ___ izar ___
11. ___ lligato ___
12. ___ idewinde ___
13. ___ obr ___
14. ___ ytho ___
15. ___ ortois ___
16. ___ hameleo ___
17. ___ guan ___
18. ___ onitor lizar ___

Birds

1. ___ wa ___
2. ___ wallo ___
3. ___ urke ___
4. ___ lbatros ___
5. ___ oos ___
6. ___ anar ___
7. ___ eacoc ___
8. ___ udgeriga ___
9. ___ iw ___
10. ___ agpi ___
11. ___ laming ___
12. ___ uc ___
13. ___ alco ___
14. ___ eagul ___
15. ___ uzzar ___
16. ___ ultur ___
17. ___ obi ___
18. ___ parro ___
19. ___ engui ___
20. ___ hicke ___
21. ___ wif ___
22. ___ elica ___

Mammals

1. ___ a ___
2. ___ ors ___
3. ___ hal ___
4. ___ eindee ___
5. ___ o ___
6. ___ ous ___
7. ___ abbi ___
8. ___ lephan ___
9. ___ p ___
10. ___ ntelop ___
11. ___ yen ___
12. ___ iraff ___
13. ___ eave ___
14. ___ ebr ___
15. ___ orill ___
16. ___ anthe ___
17. ___ oa ___
18. ___ ige ___
19. ___ angaro ___
20. ___ olphi ___
21. ___ ea ___
22. ___ ame ___

Insects

1. ___ ot ___
2. ___ eetl ___
3. ___ ermit ___
4. ___ ockroac ___
5. ___ le ___
6. ___ ocus ___
7. ___ arwi ___
8. ___ osquit ___
9. ___ as ___
10. ___ ricke ___
11. ___ ragonfl ___
12. ___ oneybe ___
13. ___ na ___
14. ___ orne ___
15. ___ ilverfis ___
16. ___ adybir ___
17. ___ ous ___
18. ___ eevi ___

Flowers

1. ___ os ___
2. ___ ais ___
3. ___ nowdro ___
4. ___ hrysanthemu ___
5. ___ il ___
6. ___ ahli ___
7. ___ luebel ___
8. ___ arnatio ___
9. ___ ans ___
10. ___ rchi ___
11. ___ egoni ___
12. ___ avende ___
13. ___ opp ___
14. ___ iole ___
15. ___ affodi ___
16. ___ unflowe ___
17. ___ ri ___
18. ___ uli ___

Add one letter to the beginning and end of these to make a word in the category.

Space and Space Travel

1. ___ art ___	2. ___ lut ___	3. ___ stronau ___	4. ___ alax ___
5. ___ ta ___	6. ___ enu ___	7. ___ upite ___	8. ___ atellit ___
9. ___ uasa ___	10. ___ ocke ___	11. ___ eptun ___	12. ___ nivers ___
13. ___ ome ___	14. ___ lane ___	15. ___ steroi ___	16. ___ paceshi ___
17. ___ oo ___	18. ___ atur ___	19. ___ ercur ___	20. ___ eteorit ___
21. ___ ar ___	22. ___ ranu ___	23. ___ unspo ___	24. ___ onstellatio ___

Elements

1. ___ odiu ___	2. ___ ilve ___	3. ___ raniu ___	4. ___ agnesiu ___
5. ___ ro ___	6. ___ oppe ___	7. ___ alciu ___	8. ___ hlorin ___
9. ___ in ___	10. ___ xyge ___	11. ___ ulphu ___	12. ___ hosphoru ___
13. ___ ol ___	14. ___ arbo ___	15. ___ itroge ___	16. ___ ydroge ___
17. ___ ea ___	18. ___ icke ___	19. ___ latinu ___	20. ___ lutoniu ___

The Weather

1. ___ inte ___	2. ___ umme ___	3. ___ hunde ___	4. ___ ightnin ___
5. ___ ros ___	6. ___ easo ___	7. ___ rough ___	8. ___ eatwav ___
9. ___ o ___	10. ___ utum ___	11. ___ ornad ___	12. ___ hermomete ___
13. ___ lou ___	14. ___ prin ___	15. ___ hirlwin ___	16. ___ emperatur ___
17. ___ ai ___	18. ___ yclon ___	19. ___ lizzar ___	20. ___ urrican ___
21. ___ no ___	22. ___ ainbo ___	23. ___ tmospher ___	24. ___ eteorolog ___

The Plant Kingdom

1. ___ actu ___	2. ___ hoo ___	3. ___ eta ___	4. ___ egetabl ___
5. ___ oo ___	6. ___ os ___	7. ___ lowe ___	8. ___ ultivat ___
9. ___ re ___	10. ___ rui ___	11. ___ hru ___	12. ___ ranc ___
13. ___ te ___	14. ___ ee ___	15. ___ olle ___	16. ___ ungu ___
17. ___ ea ___	18. ___ iche ___	19. ___ hotosynthesi ___	

The Earth's Surface and Environments

1. ___ ive ___	2. ___ ores ___	3. ___ ceber ___	4. ___ ontinen ___
5. ___ ak ___	6. ___ agoo ___	7. ___ ungl ___	8. ___ aterfal ___
9. ___ alle ___	10. ___ eser ___	11. ___ lacie ___	12. ___ ountai ___
13. ___ slan ___	14. ___ undr ___	15. ___ olcan ___	

Draw and label some things you might use to make discoveries in science.

Which is Which?

Can you match these closely related things with their correct definitions?

Andrew has kindly done the first one for you, but he would like your help with the rest. Use the clues that he has left in the brackets.

1. The digits on your hands are called <u>fingers</u> and those on your feet are called <u>toes</u>.
    (fingers and toes)

2. _____ have legs but _____ don't.
    (grubs and caterpillars)

3. _____ is a country in the south Pacific Ocean, while
    _____ includes Australia, New Zealand, Papua New
    Guinea and their associated islands. *(Australia and Australasia)*

4. _____ (like advice) is a noun while _____ (like advise) is a
    verb. *(practice and practise)*

5. _____ do not have tails while most _____ do. *(monkeys and apes)*

6. _____ have legs while _____ have flippers.
    (turtles and tortoises)

7. The area around the South Pole is called _____ while the area
    around the North Pole is called the _____. *(Antarctica and Arctic)*

8. The _____ of a song is the tune while the words are known as the
    _____. *(lyrics and melody)*

9. _____ rest with their wings lying flat while _____ rest with
    their wings held together vertically. *(moths and butterflies)*

10. In a _____ competitors must jump 10 obstacles at distances
    varying between 100 and 400 metres, but in a _____
    competitors must jump 28 obstacles and 7 water jumps over a 3 000-metre course.
    (hurdle race and steeplechase)

11. _____ are the written symbols we use for _____, which
    are the actual amounts. *(numbers and numerals)*

12. _____ is made from vegetable oils while _____ is made
    from milk. *(butter and margarine)*

13. _____ have a dry, warty skin while _____ have a
    smooth, moist skin. *(frogs and toads)*

14. A small amount of carbon is added to _____ to make
    _____. *(iron and steel)*

15. While very similiar, _____ are smaller than
    _____. _____ grow to about 2 metres while
    _____ can grow to about 4.5 metres. *(dolphins and porpoises)*

Hidden Animals

A terrible thing happened when Jim was left in charge of the zoo. When he fed the animals, he forgot to close the entrance to their enclosures. Many wandered away and became mixed up with or hidden in the words and sentences below. Please help Jim find them and return them to their enclosures before the zookeeper returns. *When you have found the animal, write it on the line provided. The number tells you how many letters in its name.*

1. kitchen (3) _____

2. indicate (3) _____

3. bullion (4) and (4) _____ _____

4. crater (3) _____

5. grapevine (3) _____

6. lassie (3) _____

7. molecule (4) _____

8. sticky (4) _____

9. crowded (4) _____

10. boxing (2) _____

11. deodorant (3) _____

12. debate (3) _____

13. blackboard (4) _____

14. scowling (3) and (3) _____ _____

15. scrabble (4) _____

16. unbearable (4) _____

17. shared (4) _____

18. selfishness (4) _____

19. Go at once! (4) _____

20. In mathematics, we learn to add and subtract. (4) _____

21. 'Give him ice,' said the waiter. (4) _____

22. To and fro goes the pendulum. (4) _____

23. Noah began to push ark animals inside when he felt some rain. (5) _____

24. 'Please do go away!' shouted Mary. (3) _____

25. In Australia, Broken Hill is one of the main producers of lead. (4) _____

26. 'Would you rather go to the beach or sew?' asked Mother. (5) _____

27. After running, Ena began to pant, her breath making small steamclouds. (7)

    _____

28. Brian Bullant eloped with his true love, Tamara Termite. (8) _____

29. Bruce bought his piano in a London keyboard shop. (6) _____

30. Suddenly, a rabbit dressed in overalls asked, 'What's up Doc?'
    'To push start a car should I leave the handbrake off?' asked the surgeon.

    (7) _____

On the back of the page, make up a few of your own hidden animals. Check the spelling of your animal's names, and the words that make them up.

Rhyming Words

Tony and Mark are very good friends. Sometimes Mark finds it difficult to understand his friend because on his planet the language they speak is similar to ours but not exactly the same. Their words rhyme with our words. See *if you can translate the words from Tony's language to ours. Do your best to spell the words correctly.*

A. **Tony's twenty favourite foods.**

1. thread and gutter = <u>bread and butter</u>

2. lake and Sydney = _____

3. raked spleens = _____

4. glum hooding = _____

5. rusted cart = _____

6. dish and whips = _____

7. taken and pegs = _____

8. hurry louder = _____

9. dried mice = _____

10. pot logs with horse = _____

11. leeches and steam = _____

12. brute ballad = _____

13. sicken poodle loop = _____

14. stork shops = _____

15. feet high = _____

16. silk Jake = _____

17. dread and gripping = _____

18. belly jabies = _____

19. ghost leaf = _____

20. tie and bees = _____

Now that you are an expert in Tony talk, write the names of these characters from nursery rhymes and tales below.

B. **Tony's favourite nursery characters.**

1. Bomb Plum = _____

2. Lack Corner = _____

3. Flee Willy Dinkie = _____

4. Go Creep = _____

5. Brother Moose = _____

6. Brittle Toy Clue = _____

7. From, From the Viper's Bun = _____

8. Lunch and Moody = _____

9. Litre Wiper (who licked a wreck of sickled lepers) = _____

10. Kiss Buffet = _____

Now for some really serious stuff. Can you identify this one below?

   Madam and Heave (Bible people) = _____

Jim loves eating. Best of all he loves to eat fruit and vegetables. When he isn't eating, he is usually thinking about food.

Just the other day he wrote out this list of favourite fruits and vegetables. Unfortunately, on that day the vowels on his typewriter had gone for a picnic with their relatives, the punctuation marks.

Put the correct vowels in the spaces to complete the words. Write Jim's secret message below.

The great secret message of Jim: _____

_____

_____

_____

f [ ] __ g

g [r] __ p __

c [ ] c __ mb __ r

__ n [ ] __ n

p __ [t] __ t __

k [ ] w __ fr __ __ t

[s] w __ d __

[ ] ppl __

__ [v] __ c __ d __

p [ ] __ ch

t __ [r] n __ p

bl __ ckb __ rr [y]

p [ ] n __ __ ppl __

t __ [m] __ t __

[p] __ rsl __ y

[ ] r __ ng __

p __ [r] sn __ p

l __ [t] t __ c __

m [ ] nd __ r __ n

b __ [n] __ n __

w __ [t] __ rm __ l __ n

s [p] __ n __ ch

c [ ] rr __ t

[r] __ spb __ rry

n __ [t]

c [ ] c __ n __ t

c __ __ l __ [f] l __ w __ r

str __ wb __ rr [y]

[ ] l __ v __

s __ ts [ ] m __

[r] h __ b __ rb

[d] __ t __

__ pr [ ] c __ t

l __ [ ] k

br __ ss __ ls spr __ __ [t]

Write the group names for the fruits or vegetables below.

1. Cox's Orange Pippin, Golden Delicious, Granny Smith: <u>a p p l e s</u>

2. King Edward, Maris Piper, Romano, Desiree: _____

3. Cherry, Beef, Money Maker: _____

4. Savoy, Chinese, Cale, Red, Spring: _____

5. Navel, Valencia, Seville: _____

6. Victoria, Early River, Santa Rosa, Czar: _____

7. William, Packham, Conference: _____

Match the answers from the word wall with their correct spaces. Colour each brick as you place its answer in a sentence.

America's	Siamese	Mexican	Portuguese	Indian
African	Victoria	German	Irish	Arctic
Indian	French	Swede	Turkish	Roman
Welsh	Chinese	Panama	Welsh	Danish

1. The _____ wave is performed by spectators in an arena by standing and raising their arms one after another.

2. The _____ tern flies around the globe.

3. The _____ Cup is a famous yacht-racing competition.

4. Chips are also called _____ fries.

5. When twins are joined together they are known as _____ twins.

6. An _____ giver is someone who gives a gift and then later asks for it to be returned.

7. When summer weather occurs after the summer season, it is called an _____ summer.

8. In the game of _____ Whispers, a message is passed from person to person in a group and the final message is compared to the original to see how much it has changed.

9. _____ rarebit is a dish of melted cheese on toast.

10. A _____ hat is made of fine straw-like material.

11. Someone who gambles but does not pay when he or she loses is said to _____ on the deal.

12. A _____ is a kind of turnip.

13. _____ blue is a type of blue-veined cheese.

14. _____ delight is a jelly like sweet, coated with icing sugar.

15. _____ measles is a contagious disease.

16. The _____ elephant has much bigger ears than the Indian elephant.

17. The _____ candle is a colourful firework.

18. A _____ man o'war resembles a jellyfish and has long, stinging tentacles.

19. _____ stew is a stew made of beef, lamb or mutton with potatoes and onions added.

20. The _____ Cross is awarded to British soldiers for acts of great bravery.

Research: Find out and write about Chang and Eng.

Activity: Play a game of _____ Whispers. By playing this game you will get some understanding of why stories that you hear second- or third-hand are often very far from the truth.

In each group below all the words except one have something in common. Circle and colour or highlight the word that is out of place in each group. The first one has been done for you.

1.   comic, (library,) novel, dictionary, newspaper
2.   watch, hour, second, day, minute
3.   microscope, stethoscope, glasses, binoculars, telescope
4.   pawn, king, draught, knight, queen
5.   kangaroo, koala, dingo, wombat, horse
6.   nose, eyebrow, wig, ear, forehead, chin
7.   cat, piglet, foal, calf, puppy
8.   nought, chicken, duck, love, zero
9.   new, dew, few, sew, stew, chew
10. screw cap, jar lid, ring-pull tab, steering wheel, doorknob, radio dial
11. influenza, cancer, measles, malaria, chickenpox
12. Mayday! (from French m'aider), Help! Hello! SOS!
13. river, stream, lake, brook, waterfall
14. cricket, golf, tennis, soccer, ice hockey, baseball

15. swallow, penguin, sparrow, magpie, seagull
16. ant, worm, pig, bird, fly, centipede
17. zebra, bee, ladybird, tiger
18. Berlin, Manchester, London, Liverpool, Leeds
19. shirt, coat, trousers, jacket, jumper
20. pine, rose, beech, oak, willow
21. sheep, cow, dog, horse, goat
22. square, triangle, circle, rectangle, pentagon
23. Mr Toad, Donald Duck, Black Beauty, Robin Hood, Peter Rabbit
24. knee, shin, elbow, ankle, wrist
25. car, tram, bus, truck, van
26. refrigerator, typewriter, freezer, toaster, food processor

27. snail, whole egg, fried egg, turtle, tortoise
28. triangle, cube, sphere, pyramid, cylinder, hemisphere
29. trumpet, violin, guitar, banjo, harp
30. cobra, python, tiger snake, death adder, taipan
31. nail, hammer, screwdriver, chisel, hacksaw
32. crab, starfish, lobster, crayfish
33. £10, £15, £20, £50, £100
34. skin, bark, peel, fur, seed
35. stingray, tuna, catfish, dolphin, shark
36. add, fraction, subtract, multiply, divide
37. Henry VIII, Michael Jackson, Queen Victoria, Elizabeth II
38. silver, gold, diamond, copper, tin
39. mattress, pillow, pyjamas, blanket, quilt
40. pelican, goose, swan, horse

Association

Circle and colour or highlight the two words in each group that are most associated with the first word.

1. SCHOOL - gravel, children, coal, pencils, cabbage
2. GRAPE - tree, vine, seeds, pink, bark
3. HUNDRED - year, century, second, centimetre, noses
4. GOLDILOCKS - pigs, wolf, bears, dragon, porridge
5. DODO - fly, bird, swift, extinct, Canada
6. CHRISTMAS - Delilah, eggs, manger, bunny, Wise Men
7. EGYPT - pyramid, sphinx, kangaroo, Europe, icebergs
8. HELICOPTER - wings, blades, outerspace, runway, hovering
9. TENNIS - racquet, rattle, wallet, tantrum, ball
10. APE - monkey, gorilla, tail, chimpanzee, Tarzan
11. SPACE - green men, stars, fish, cowboys, asteroids
12. EAGLE - golden, eyrie, fur, Antarctica, paws
13. MAIL - female, stamp, file, Adam, letter
14. ISLAM - Buddha, mosque, Hindu, Muslim, Confucius
15. OLYMPICS - marbles, fiddlesticks, Greece, hopscotch, marathon
16. BEACH - winter, sand, snakes, towel, cactus
17. BALLET - elephant, leaf, tutu, audience, concrete mixer
18. RUBBER - nails, tree, tapper, chewing gum, magnet
19. ESKIMO - Greenland, Antarctica, Fiji, penguins, igloo
20. SPIDER - insect, web, arachnid, sting, singing
21. ORE - boat, metal, rowing, mineral, either
22. COURT - newspaper, judge, jury, bird, flying fish
23. CRICKET - slam dunk, stump, freestyle, discus, Lords.
24. UNITED
    KINGDOM - Mersey, Amazon, Mississippi, Nile, Severn
25. BAWL - basket, tennis, cry, dancing, tears
26. ROOF - blinds, floorboards, tiles, plaster, thatch
27. NOAH - animals, Goliath, Easter, Santa, flood
28. JOURNALIST - headline, comics, crossword, article, fairytale
29. SHOE - stomach, leather, tree, chair, heel
30. SHIRT - trousers, collar, sleeve, zip, socks
31. FISH - custard, dolphin, scales, chips, gills
32. FLOWER - trunk, stem, branches, petals, lawn
33. COMPUTER - keyboard, saw, cursor, Einstein, teeth
34. SPECTACLES - shoebox, lens, wrist, rims, telephone
35. JAPAN - Beijing, kimono, origami, hot dogs, jungles
36. HORSE - trunk, stable, wheels, whinny, horns
37. FOOT - toe, knee, thigh, shin, ankle
38. YACHT - motor, oars, propeller, mast, sails
39. SHEEP - cotton, shearer, wool, carnivorous, boots
40. MUSIC - siren, soprano, spaghetti, compact disc, sneeze

Spaghetti Words

Do you like spaghetti? Lisa loves it. Apart from eating it she finds many other uses for it (wrapping gifts, hanging very light pictures etc.). Yesterday, when she was writing out some famous threes, she mixed them up as you will see below. She then used different coloured bits of spaghetti to link them properly. *If your teacher doesn't let you use spaghetti, use different coloured pencils to link the three words together.*

Terms Used in Sport

1.	leg	Cricket	wicket
2.	on	and	one
3.	hole	row	shot
4.	on	before	Club
5.	putting	your	boundary
6.	Marylebone	in	forward
7.	backhand	the	bowled
8.	front	for	race
9.	three	passing	marks
10.	caught	-legged	par

Famous People

1.	Good	da	King
2.	Sir	Luther	Wells
3.	John	of	Nottingham
4.	Leonardo	Winston	Bruce
5.	H	Isaac	Vinci
6.	Ludwig	King	Churchill
7.	Martin	the	Beethoven
8.	Sir	the	Wenceslas
9.	Sheriff	G	Newton
10.	Joan	Von	Baptist
11.	Robert	the	Arc
12.	Alfred	of	Great

Well-known Trios

1.	stiff	line	or mineral
2.	here	Melchior	and Louie
3.	Flopsy	there	and sinker
4.	sugar	upper	and barrel
5.	hook	Dewey	and Balthazar
6.	Caspar	stock	and Cottontail
7.	Huey	nose	lip
8.	lock	vegetable	and throat
9.	ear	spice	and everywhere
10.	animal	Mopsy	and all things nice

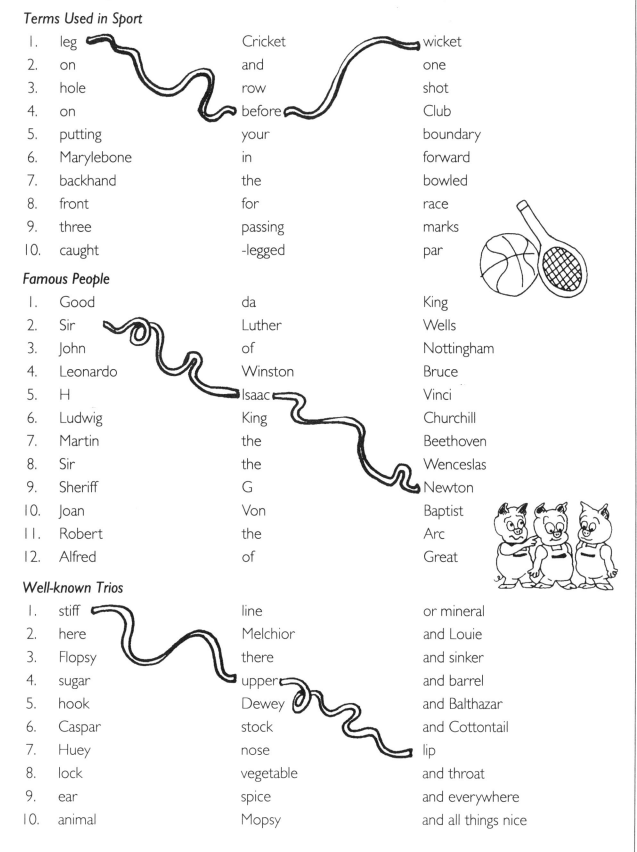

Choose an ending from those given below to finish each group of words.

horse	pool	fall	ship	maid	bag	cake	bat	nail	ball
time	way	coat	bird	fly	berry	sense	match	dance	hat
train	side	boots	star	chop	case	chair	worm	paper	cast

1. sea, rocking, Trojan, race: _h o r s e_
2. fruit, baseball, cricket, vampire: _____
3. broad, fore, plaster, over: _____
4. freight, electric, steam, camel: _____
5. birthday, fish, wedding, fairy: _____
6. square, belly, tap, rain: _____
7. swimming, rock, whirl: _____
8. finger, toe, roofing: _____
9. green, horse, sand, house: _____
10. news, wall, tissue, carbon: _____
11. in, out, be, sea: _____
12. cricket, football, mis, safety, test: _____
13. top, rain, bowler, sun: _____
14. football, Puss in, Wellington: _____
15. over, trench, rain, waist: _____
16. day, night, summer, lunch: _____
17. lamb, karate, pork: _____
18. gas, hand, sand, punch: _____
19. water, down, rain, free: _____
20. sailing, battle, space, tall: _____
21. book, earth, glow: _____
22. brief, book, court, suit: _____
23. road, cause, motor, gang: _____
24. lady, black, humming, whirly: _____
25. high, deck, rocking: _____
26. house, milk, upstairs, chamber: _____
27. shooting, falling, pop, film: _____
28. foot, basket, net, volley: _____
29. common, horse, sixth, non: _____
30. rasp, goose, black, straw: _____

Extension: *Can you find endings to these?*

1. Donald, Daffy, Daisy, mallard: _____
2. black, lock, silver, tin: _____
3. hair, upper, square, crew: _____
4. fast, junk, health, brain: _____
5. talkback, two-way, transistor: _____

The same word can be used in each pair to complete the first word and begin the second. A clue is given to help you. *Put the correct word to complete each puzzle pair then write the complete words in the spaces provided.*

Bird __pelican__   peli(C A N)ada   Country __Canada__

Greedy _____   sel(__ __ __)erman   Angler _____

Big person _____   gi(__ __)enna   Aerial _____

Small house _____   cott(__ __ __)nt   Spy _____

Send overseas _____ ex(__ __ __ __)er   Carrier of luggage _____

Sport _____   tenn(__ __)land   Land in water _____

Leave _____   de(__ __ __ __)ner   Associate _____

Woodland _____   fo(__ __ __ __)less   Unsettled _____

In the open _____   out(__ __ __ __)line   Sportsfield marking _____

Mend _____   rep(__ __ __)craft   Flying machine _____

Not fresh _____   st(__ __ __)rt   Lively _____

Current _____   re(__ __ __ __)urion   Roman Commander in charge of 100 men _____

Going forever _____ end(__ __ __ __)on   School period _____

Fish _____   flo(__ __ __ __ __)stand Grasp the meaning _____

Sport _____   foot(__ __ __ __)erina   Dancer _____

Vegetable _____   car(__ __ __)ate   Revolve _____

Bird _____   spar(__ __ __)dy   Disorderly _____

Rider _____   cyc(__ __ __ __)en   Hear _____

Business partnership _____   comp(__ __ __)body   No particular person _____

Earth _____   pla(__ __ __)ball   Sport _____

Order _____   comm(__ __ __)ersen   Author of fairy tales _____

Plant bed _____   gar(__ __ __)tist   Tooth doctor _____

To be present _____ att(__ __ __)anger   Put someone in peril _____

Error _____   mis(__ __ __ __)away   Fast food _____

Body part _____   he(__ __ __)ist   Painter _____

Hut _____   cab(__ __)sect   Animal _____

Starting Words

Find words with each beginning that fit the clues. Check your spelling with a dictionary.

STAR TREK

This STAR is the beginning - S T A R T

This STAR is what happens if you go without food for too long - _____

This STAR is a type of bird - _____

This STAR is the right-hand side of a ship - _____

This STAR means to surprise - _____

This STAR is used to stiffen material - _____

This STAR is the name given to you when you look at the stars - _____

CATS IN THE BELFRY

This CAT is a book listing things for sale - _____

This CAT was used in warfare many years ago to hurl large stones - _____

This CAT is a rotating firework - _____

This CAT speeds up a chemical reaction - _____

This CAT will grow into a butterfly - _____

This CAT is a large church - _____

This CAT is the name of a religion - _____

This CAT is a two-hulled boat - _____

This CAT is a disaster - _____

This CAT is a collective name for cows - _____

ANT ATTACK

This ANT is the Southern polar icecap - _____

This ANT is connected to your television - _____

This ANT is a type of gazelle - _____

This ANT is a national song - _____

This ANT is used to kill germs - _____

This ANT is taken to neutralise poisons - _____

This ANT is an island in the West Indies - _____

This ANT is the name given to Australia and New Zealand - _____

EARLY MAN

This MAN is another name for a handcuff - _____

This MAN is the boss in a bank - _____

This MAN is a citrus fruit - _____

This MAN is a tropical fruit with a large furry seed in the middle - _____

This MAN is a pear-shaped musical instrument - _____

This MAN is used to display clothes - _____

This MAN is a large stately house - _____

This MAN is the making of goods - _____

Odd One Out

By unjumbling the words below you will find an 'odd one out' in each group. *Write the words out, then circle the 'odd one out'.*

T A S N	Stan	In this example 'Rover' is the odd one out
J M I	Jim	because the others are all boy's names
O T M	Tom	
R E V R O	Rover	

1. E B E _____
   T N A _____
   R D Y _____
   Y F L _____

2. A H D N _____
   O O F T _____
   I L O N _____
   E N S O _____

3. W R O B N _____
   L K C B A _____
   Y L E J L _____
   N R E G E _____

4. H R C I A _____
   A L B E T _____
   O L S T O _____
   R K I D N _____

5. Y U R B G _____
   S O M U E _____
   S N E N T I _____
   C S R E C O _____

6. L I T P S A C _____
   E C O F E F _____
   A C C O O _____
   A O E L M N E D _____

7. E T I K T N _____
   Y U P P P _____
   T L G P I E _____
   L W O E B _____

8. R K S I T _____
   O L B S E U _____
   S R E D S _____
   C M N E E T _____

9. M R A L S E B _____
   K U C R T _____
   N I T A R _____
   L I Y C B C E _____

10. L E C I P N A _____
    L U E S A G L _____
    R N S O I G N _____
    K T S R O _____

11. T L I A Y _____
    I P N A O _____
    R P T U M E T _____
    L T E U F _____

12. E B B C A A G _____
    R P O R S W A _____
    C E U T L T E _____
    N P I S C A H _____

13. N U O D P _____
    E I R R V _____
    K O R O B _____
    P A S W M _____

14. O T C R T A R _____
    Z L O R E D L B U _____
    H A R S E V R T E _____
    M E L I T H B _____

15. E U C B H T R _____
    C M L A E _____
    B E R A K _____
    R E O C R G _____

Matching Pairs

Join the matching pairs as shown below. Use different colours to match each pair.

A. **Hat** / **Country**

Hat	Country
fez	India
turban	Mexico
sombrero	Turkey
bowler	Australia
beret	England
cork hat	France

F. **Part** / **Whole**

Part	Whole
electron	bell
crust	blood
tongue	copper
plasma	atom
bronze	unicorn
horn	pie

B. **Slang** / **Job**

Slang	Job
Jack Tar	actor
Bobby	carpenter
brickie	sailor
ham	magistrate
beak	bricklayer
chippie	Policeman

G. **Animal** / **Associated Country**

Animal	Associated Country
kangaroo	India
llama	Peru
mongoose	China
yak	Borneo
panda	Australia
orang-utan	Tibet

C. **Person** / **What they collect**

Person	What they collect
Numismatist	stamps
Philatelist	records
Discophile	coins
Phillumenist	books
Lepidopterist	butterflies
Bibliophile	matchbox tops

H. **Sport** / **Country of Origin**

Sport	Country of Origin
sumo wrestling	USA
baseball	Scotland
cricket	Japan
polo	Persia/India
golf	Ireland
hurling	England

D. **Character** / **What it is**

Character	What it is
Black Beauty	rag doll
Andy Pandy	puppet
Pinocchio	horse
Moby Dick	tiger
Shere Khan	pig
Babe	whale

I. **Bone** / **Location**

Bone	Location
femur	hips
skull	forearm
pelvis	wrist
radius and ulna	thigh
tarsus	head
metacarpal	ankle

E. **Inventor** / **Invention/Advancement**

Inventor	Invention/Advancement
Edison	radio
Bell	television
Baird	light bulb
Marconi	movable printing type
Gutenberg	motor car
Galileo	helicopter
Sikorsky	telephone
Benz	telescope

J. **Historical Figure** / **Associated Country**

Historical Figure	Associated Country
Napoleon	England
Cleopatra	France
St Patrick	USA
Simon Bolivar	Egypt
George Washington	Venezuela
Ghandi	Czechoslovakia
Alfred the Great	Ireland
Good King Wenceslas	India

Word Chains

Extend these word chains to ten links. Each link in the word chain must begin with the last letter of the word preceding it.

Example:

Countries: Brazil - Lebanon - Norway - Yemen - Nepal - Laos - Spain - Nigeria - Austria - Australia

Boys' Names: John - _____

_____

_____

Cars: _____

_____

_____

Girls' Names: _____

_____

_____

Plants: _____

_____

_____

Animals: _____

_____

_____

Towns and Cities: _____

_____

_____

Things at School: _____

_____

_____

Make up some categories yourself then complete word chains for them.

_____

_____

_____

_____

_____

_____

Try to work out the familiar word, phrase or figure of speech below.

s t a i r s		R E A D I N G
Upstairs		

o n e e m r t e	**n e s s** **Her Royal**	*c y c l e* *c y c l e* *c y c l e*

LOND **BRIDGE**	hat hat hat	**standing** **mis**

chance	wolf	*ASLEEP* o o

B B B B B B B B B B B B B BB B B B B B B B B B	**arm** **deodorant**	3 0 ° ✓

Colour the pictures when you have finished or while you are thinking. See if you can make up any of these yourself.

What's My Number?

Choose from the numbers below to complete each phrase or sentence. Colour each answer block as you find the answer.

ten	seventy	two	twenty-one	three	three	four	nine	one	ten
two	seven	hundred	seven	three	five	three	two	twelve	
three	four	thousand	three	seven	three	nine	seven	four	

1. You sprinkle fairycakes with coloured _____s and _____s.

2. Many people enjoy _____ pin bowling.

3. The city of Rome was built on _____ hills.

4. When Jesus was born he was visited by _____ wise men.

5. To be elaborately dressed is to be 'dressed up to the _____s'.

6. _____ is said to be company while _____ is said to be a crowd.

7. The Colossus of Rhodes was one of the _____ wonders of the world.

8. A small quiet town is sometimes called a _____ -horse town.

9. A _____ -poster is a bed with curtains around it.

10. Moses received the _____ Commandments on Mount Sinai.

11. The _____ bears were very fond of porridge.

12. Pontoon or _____'s is the name of a card game.

13. There are said to be _____ deadly sins.

14. A _____ o'clock shadow appears on a man with a heavy beard.

15. A car driver may turn around using a _____ -point turn.

16. A _____-way is a radio which you can listen to and send messages from.

17. Christ had _____ close followers.

18. A cat is said to have _____ lives.

19. A _____ -wheel drive car is necessary when driving over very rough country.

20. _____ blind mice had their tails cut off by a farmer's wife.

21. Someone three score years and ten is the equivalent of
    _____ years old.

22. A _____ -leaf clover is said to bring luck to its finder.

23. In the fairytale, Snow White lived with _____ dwarfs.

24. A person who is _____ -faced can not be trusted.

25. The _____ little pigs were almost made into bacon burgers by a wolf.

26. At a picnic you might compete in a _____ -legged race.

Roman Numerals

Bruce has been doing so much work on Roman numerals lately that he sometimes forgets himself when writing and writes the value of the Roman numeral rather than the letter in some words. For example; in one of his stories he recently wrote: 'I 50 + 1 + ke to 100 + 50 + 1 + 1 000 + b trees'. What he meant, of course, was: 'I like to climb trees'.

Can you correct his spelling list before the teacher sees it? Oh yes, if you haven't been doing lots of Roman numerals lately, they are shown below in the box.

I = 1	V = 5	X = 10	L = 50	C = 100	D = 500	M = 1 000

1 000 + 1 + 10 = <u>M I X</u> .

1 000 + 1 + 50 + 500 = _____

100 + 1 + 5 + 1 + 50 = _____

100 + 1 + 5 + 1 + 100 = _____

500 + 1 + 1 000 + E = _____

1 000 + 1 + 100 + E = _____

50 + 1 + 500 = _____

5 + 1 + 1 000 = _____

5 + 1 + 100 + E = _____

1 000 + 1 + 50 + 50 = _____

E + 50 + 1 + 10 + 1 + R = _____

500 + E + 100 + 1 + 1 000 + A + 50 = _____

50 + 1 + 5 + 1 + 500 = _____

100 + RO + 100 + O + 500 + 1 + 50 + E = _____

50 + 1 + 1 000 + 1 + T = _____

Place the words you have made into the correct sentences below.

1. Lisa made a lovely cake using her mother's cake <u>M I X</u> .
2. According to a well-known song, you should never smile at a _____.
3. Grain is ground into flour at a _____.
4. It is dangerous to drive faster than the speed _____.
5. James Watt learnt that steam could be used to do work when he saw it lift up the _____ of his mother's kettle.
6. The library was located in the _____ centre of the town.
7. In the USA a ten-cent coin is called a _____.
8. Stan says he has invented an _____ that turns cement into gold.
9. A war between people of the same country is called a _____ war.
10. *Mickey* and *Minnie* were delighted when they were paid a visit by the holidaying three blind _____.
11. The carpenter used a _____ to hold the piece of wood.
12. Adam was _____ when he found a knot in his best piece of string.
13. We use a _____ number system.
14. An energetic person is said to be full of _____.
15. Superman's secret identity is _____ -mannered reporter, Clark Kent.

Name-dropping

Change one letter in each name below to make the word with the meaning shown.
Write your new word in the space provided.

Boys' Names

1. Bruce = a beast _____ brute _____
2. Terry = a boat _____
3. Mark = a tree's skin _____
4. Brian = a prickly bush _____
5. Bert = not straight _____
6. James = slang word for girls _____
7. Grant = a big person _____
8. Aaron = a nobleman _____
9. Lance = the tango _____
10. Roger = common dog's name _____
11. Billy = hurtful person _____
12. Joe = work _____
13. Davy = an armed force _____
14. Harry = Laurel's partner _____
15. Barry = a fruit family _____
16. Gene = a man _____
17. Walter = restaurant servant _____
18. Warren = prison officer _____
19. Luke = nobleman _____
20. Charles = what a bull does _____
21. Dennis = a sport _____
22. Frank = sipped _____
23. Greg = a colour _____
24. Cary = to bother _____
25. Mike = rodents _____
26. Alan = scheme _____
27. Fred = no charge _____
28. Neil = claw _____
29. Stan = a sun _____
30. Tony = very small _____
31. Cory = apple centre _____
32. Shane = form of a thing _____
33. Sidney = organ of the body _____
34. Tim = worn around the neck _____
35. Ross = plant grown on stones _____
36. Romeo = cowboy show _____
37. Doug = medicinal substance _____
38. Clive = type of cooking oil _____

Girls' Names

Rose = facial feature _____ nose _____
Tina = a fish _____
Jean = nasty _____
Marge = big _____
Dawn = grass plot _____
Lulu = African tribe _____
Ann = little insect _____
Mary = planet _____
Jane = not mad _____
Jenny = old name for 1p _____
Pat = large rodent _____
Peggy = long legs _____
Jill = a tablet _____
Mabel = name tag _____
Joan = to whinge _____
Angela = heavenly beings _____
Sue = our star _____
Jan = sweet preserved fruit _____
Nancy = elaborate _____
Fay = overweight _____
Kelly = wobbly dessert _____
Wendy = breezy _____
Betty = a wharf _____
Megan = started _____
Ruth = to hurry _____
Bessy = bullying _____
Tracy = to draw over _____
Lisa = to lean over _____
Kerry = happy _____
Lucy = fortune _____
Kim = edge _____
Sally = not sweet _____
Olive = not dead _____
Ivy = very cold _____
Polly = Christmas plant _____
Wanda = black and white bear _____
Heather = plume of a bird _____
Lizzy = giddy _____

Words in Words

Find the word related to the topic that is hidden in each bigger word.
The number of letters in your hidden word is shown in brackets.
Write the hidden word in the space provided.

Food

impeachment (5)	_____	screaming (5)	_____
appearance (4)	_____	repeat (3)	_____
abundant (3)	_____	pieces (3)	_____
revealing (4)	_____	scornful (4)	_____
priceless (4)	_____	champion (3)	_____
beggar (3)	_____	floats (4)	_____

Body Parts

harmless (3)	_____	chairperson (4)	_____
chandelier (4)	_____	aching (4)	_____
asking (4)	_____	fearful (3)	_____
slippery (3)	_____	bribery (3)	_____
washing (4)	_____	plunger (4)	_____
delivery (5)	_____	shipwrecked (3)	_____

Boys' Names

atomic (3)	_____	Timbuktu (3)	_____
wasted (3)	_____	inside (3)	_____
Scotland (4)	_____	librarian (3)	_____
incompetent (4)	_____	bricklayer (4)	_____
understand (4)	_____	front (3)	_____
broken (3)	_____	silence (3)	_____
stern (3)	_____	supermarket (4)	_____
destroyer (4)	_____	victorious (6)	_____
unbalanced (4)	_____ and (5) _____		
convinced (3)	_____, (5) _____ and (2) _____		

Girls' Names

tissues (3)	_____	adorable (4)	_____
truthful (4)	_____	civilisation (4)	_____
impatient (3)	_____	disgraceful (5)	_____
suntanned (4)	_____	harmonicas (6)	_____
intestinal (4)	_____	radar (3)	_____
unscathed (4)	_____	revenge (3)	_____

Animals

indicate (3)	_____	scowling (3)	_____
crater (3)	_____	sunglasses (3)	_____
pavilion (4)	_____	feeling (3)	_____
blackboard (4)	_____	stealing (4)	_____
lichens (3)	_____	mother (4)	_____
debate (3)	_____	grapefruit (3)	_____
wrench (4)	_____	molecules (4)	_____

Words in Words II

Many of our words contain smaller words. For example; the words SCATTER, INDICATOR, CATASTROPHE and EDUCATION all contain the word 'CAT'.
Write four words containing each smaller word on the lines provided below.

1. king _____
2. car _____
3. tin _____
4. and _____
5. log _____
6. ten _____
7. can _____
8. ear _____
9. old _____
10. too _____
11. late _____
12. eve _____
13. rink _____
14. bin _____
15. fat _____
16. war _____
17. cow _____
18. hat _____
19. man _____
20. rust _____
21. low _____
22. out _____
23. her _____
24. but _____
25. our _____
26. mat _____
27. ant _____
28. row _____
29. ape _____
30. top _____

Find some small words that make up at least three other words; show them below.

_____

_____

_____

_____

Long and Short Vowels

Andrew's spelling is improving. He still mixes up long and short vowels, however. His mother has bought him two huge socks to sort them. Help him do this before his mother gets home.

Words: back, take, cake, sack, bit, kit, bite, bone, lone, home, grub, fog, sit, white, tack, date, gate, dog, bake, lack, fit, rake, hit, rack, lake, make, wake, lit, cone, pit, phone, kite, tone, state, hate, tub, bog, cub, late, cube, tube, sat, hat, mate, fat, hum, bag, ham, like

Short Vowels	Long Vowels

Do you think you can help Andrew work out a rule to help him with long and short vowels?

Syllables

You will find it easier to spell some words if you break them into syllables. When you say words at normal speed you will find that many have naturally-occurring breaks. One way to detect the syllables is to clap the breaks as you say the words. Say the words at normal speed. If you slow down you might tend to put in syllables that aren't really there. Some words are made up of only one syllable.

Example: dog = one syllable

elephant = three syllables   el ~ e ~ phant

The words below have been broken into syllables but the syllables are jumbled. *Unjumble the syllables then write the words.*

A.   *Things you do at school.*

1.   ling ~ spel = __SPEL__ + __LING__ = __SPELLING__ .

2.   ting ~ wri ~ hand = _____ + _____ + _____ = _____

3.   tu ~ tion ~ punc ~ a = _____ + _____ + _____ + _____ = _____

4.   hen ~ com ~ sion ~ pre = _____ + _____ + _____ + _____ = _____

5.   mat ~ e ~ ics ~ math = _____ + _____ + _____ + _____ = _____

6.   me ~ o ~ try ~ ge = _____ + _____ + _____ + _____ = _____

7.   ig ~ in ~ vest ~ a ~ tion = _____ + _____ + _____ + _____ + _____ = _____

8.   cul ~ tions ~ cal ~ a = _____ + _____ + _____ + _____ = _____

B.   *These are places Peter visited and things he saw in space.*

1.   to ~ plu = _____ + _____ = _____

2.   cu ~ mer ~ ry = _____ + _____ + _____ = _____

3.   pit ~ ju ~ er = _____ + _____ + _____ = _____

4.   ra ~ u ~ nus = _____ + _____ + _____ = _____

5.   la ~ stel ~ con ~ tions = _____ + _____ + _____ + _____ = _____

6.   ax ~ gal ~ ies = _____ + _____ + _____ = _____

7.   er ~ ast ~ oid = _____ + _____ + _____ = _____

8.   e ~ or ~ met = _____ + _____ + _____ = _____

9.   ro ~ ast ~ nauts = _____ + _____ + _____ = _____

C.   *These words mean 'big'*

1.   men ~ tre ~ dous = _____ + _____ + _____ = _____

2.   mous ~ nor ~ e = _____ + _____ + _____ = _____

3.   loss ~ co ~ al = _____ + _____ + _____ + _____ = _____

4.   gan ~ gi ~ tic = _____ + _____ + _____ = _____

5.   nom ~ tro ~ cal ~ as ~ i = _____ + _____ + _____ + _____ + _____ = _____

6.   um ~ ous ~ vol ~ in = _____ + _____ + _____ + _____ = _____

7.   stan ~ sub ~ tial = _____ + _____ + _____ = _____

8.   ten ~ ex ~ sive = _____ + _____ + _____ = _____

Building Blocks

Christmas - The Magi

The words related to the topic can be found in blocks in the puzzle. Words read letter to letter in any direction except diagonally. No letter is shared by words. One example has been done for you. *Colour answer blocks that connect one another different colours.*

M	R	E	N	S	E	S	E	H	S	H	R
C	R	C	H	O	D	S	E	S	T	S	A
K	I	N	R	O	W	I	R	A	O	C	K
N	M	Y	R	G	G	N	A	H	B	S	I
A	H	I	O	**G**	**O**	I	P	U	R	G	N
R	C	J	R	T	**L**	K	S	N	I	L	L
F	L	A	Y	W	**D**	Y	A	D	R	T	I
B	E	N	R	E	L	B	C	D	E	N	A
A	M	U	A	E	V	A	B	S	P	E	S
L	T	A	N	E	B	A	L	P	I	N	G
I	H	A	A	F	Y	N	A	H	K	I	M
E	S	Z	A	R	T	H	R	E	E	T	Y

FRANKINCENSE   MYRRH
THREE KINGS   GOLD
BRILLIANT   GOOD
STOCKINGS   WISE
BALTHAZAR   ASHES
EPIPHANY
LA BEFANA
MELCHIOR
BABY KING
HUNDREDS
JANUARY
TWELVE
CASPAR

Use words from the list to fill the gaps below. Fourteen letters are not used; they can be unjumbled to make a message.

Most of you probably know the song 'The _____ Days of Christmas'. These days were
1.
once all holidays. The last day on 6 _____, is also known as the _____. This
2.   3.
day commemorates the visit of the _____ to the Christ Child. These _____
4.   5.
men named _____, _____ and _____
6.   7.   8.
followed a _____ star across deserts and plains seeking a _____ whose
9.   10.
coming had been prophesied _____ of years before. To honour the Christ Child, each
11.
brought with him a gift. One gave the precious metal, _____. Another gave
12.
_____, a fragrant-smelling substance that comes from trees. The third gave
13.
_____, a sweet-smelling ointment.
14.
In Italy, a popular story is told about _____, an old woman who was visited by the wise
15.
men as they made their journey. She meant to follow them but was left behind. It is said that to this
day she still seeks the wondrous child of whom they spoke. When she visits the houses of
_____ children she fills up their _____ with toys and sweets. Bad children,
16.   17.
alas, have theirs filled with _____.
18.

Write the fourteen leftover letters here: _____

Write the special message they make when unjumbled here (in colours):

_____

Interesting Words and Sayings

English is a wonderful language. There are many ways of saying things. Perhaps the reason for this great variety is because English has developed from many other languages. At different times Britain was invaded by Italy (ancient Rome), Germany, Scandinavia and France. Each of these invaders added to the language.

Many words and expressions have an interesting story behind them. Here are some of them.

A **baker's dozen** means thirteen. Many years ago, bakers were severely punished if their loaves were underweight. Loaves were usually weighed in batches of twelve. Many bakers added an extra loaf to make sure their batch wasn't underweight.

To **get the sack** means to lose your job. In earlier times, workers usually used their own tools when working at a factory. These would be left in a sack at the workplace. When the worker left the job, the sack and tools would be taken with him.

A **jeep** is a vehicle well known for being able to be driven across very rough country. It was first made by the US army for use during World War II and was called a GP vehicle (GP for general purpose). People shortened these initials to the word 'jeep'.

When we speak about **soap operas** today we mean television serials that dramatise everyday life. Perhaps you watch some of these. The term comes from the early days of radio when there were many such serials. Soap companies were the major sponsors, because of this, they came to be called soap operas.

You may say **bless you** to someone when he or she sneezes. This custom comes from the 1600s. It was believed that someone's soul left his or her body for a short time during a sneeze. By saying 'God bless you', people believed that the soul would be protected from harm during the short time it left the sneezer's body.

If we call someone **posh** we mean they are elegant and fashionable. This word comes from the initials for 'port-side out, starboard home'. People wealthy enough to travel frequently by ship from Britain to Asia knew it was best to book their cabins on the port-side (left) on the journey there and on the starboard-side (right) on the journey back. These cabins would be on the side most shaded from the sun.

An **assassin** is a murderer who kills a prominent person. This word comes from the Arabic word 'hashshashin' meaning a person who eats hashish. Some ruthless people who wanted a political enemy killed would influence weak-minded people to do this for them by feeding them the drug hashish. While in their drugged state, they believed promises such as a place close to God in heaven as a reward. Not in their right minds, the assassins did what was asked of them.

---

1. See if you can find out the meanings and origins of the following words.

   (a) pipe down _____

   (b) scapegoat _____

   (c) gibberish _____

   (d) pleased as punch _____

   (e) codswallop _____

2. List the names of as many soap operas as you can. _____

_____

Multiple Meanings

Some words have a number of meanings. For example, one word can be used with these meanings: 'what glue does'; 'a piece of wood'; 'another word used for a golf club'.

The word **stick** has these meanings. *Find the words that fit the meanings below.*

1. (a) not heavy

    (b) not dark

    (c) what you do when you strike a match _____

2. (a) a small amount

    (b) steel piece that goes in the horse's mouth

    (c) what the dog did when Karl tried to pat it _____

3. (a) a round toy

    (b) a dance

    (c) a single delivery by the bowler in cricket _____

4. (a) a tasty seed with a hard shell

    (b) something that is fitted onto a bolt

    (c) slang word for a person's head _____

5. (a) not in danger

    (b) a strong box in which money is kept _____

6. (a) a colour

    (b) a round fruit _____

7. (a) aeroplanes do this

    (b) a small winged insect

    (c) what a kite does _____

8. (a) to joke

    (b) a slang word for child

    (c) a young goat _____

9. (a) to manage something (like a company)

    (b) a score in cricket

    (c) to move quickly _____

10. (a) the highest point in something

    (b) a spinning toy _____

11. (a) a cobbler mends shoes on one of these

    (b) to stay in being for a long time

    (c) at the end _____

12. (a) a month

    (b) how soldiers move in a procession _____

13. (a) to go without food for a long time

    (b) speedy _____

14. (a) a metal

    (b) an appliance used in pressing clothes

    (c) a golf club with a slanted metal head _____

15. (a) coming directly after first

    (b) one-sixtieth of a minute _____

Interesting Words Worksheet - page 2.

Exercise A - 1. Latin 2. Greek 3. Greek 4. German 5. Greek 6. Aztec 7. Latin 8. USA.

Exercise B - 1. the Romans 2. people believed they stole butter 3. Magellan's ship was becalmed on it 4. self-contained underwater breathing apparatus.

Exercise C - teacher to correct.

Exercise D - 1. junction 2. Portuguese 3. Aztecs 4. boundary 5. salamander.

Add-a-Word - page 3.

1. bin 2. bus 3. then 4. Scot 5. pray 6. gill 7. hand 8. Fred 9. bone 10. slow 11. farm 12. self 13. bark 14. drip 15. heel 16. pink 17. space 18. pants 19. train 20. chair 21. string 22. chum 23. brush 24. sparrow 25. driver 26. clamber 27. thunder 28. thump 29. slips 30. swings.

Our Colourful Language - page 4.

```
G B L A C Y E R G T B E
R E E N K M W H O U L U
Y E L W C A T K I A R
P U L I A Y T T C N N O
R R O T T V E E A T G K
E P W H E N R D L H E N
D L S G B L A W B E P I
C E T R E A R F P A T R
R H R E E C G B E E D A
E E K A N K R L U R L L
S A R T E D E E E C O E
C E N T A T H N H O U S
```

1. blue 2. Red Crescent 3. red tape 4. greenhouse 5. yellow streak 6. black cat 7. blue collar 8. orange, 9. green 10. green with envy 11. in the pink 12. grey matter 13. Black Death 14. Purple Heart 15. white dwarf 16. black out.

Double Words - page 5.

```
U T A K N O R T H N O R
T U C C J T M B O N E T
N B K A U U U C N B D H
A E R J B M T H O O A B
C A B B J U B O O N P N
N Y O E R Y O G C H O E
A E O O I T Y A P O M D
C A B O E O O G O O P A
O Y E G E M T A P M O B
G O N E W T A R T A R E
T G I E A O M T S E T S
I N T G G G A W A G G A
```

1. Tintin 2. jub jub 3. tum tum 4. Baden Baden 5. Tse tse 6. bonbon 7. Wagga Wagga 8. boo-boo 9. aye aye 10. yo-yo 11. gee-gee 12. tom-tom 13. north-north 14. choo choo 15. beri-beri 16. tutu 17. go-go, cancan 18. pom pom, ack ack 19. tartar 20. Pago Pago.

Double Trouble - page 6.

slimmer, stagger, ruffian, barrier, skilled, skipped/skidded, battle, baffle, buggy, bunny,

sudden, puzzle, suffer, summer, raffle, bigger, bidder, million, fussier, funnier, needle

dapple, dabble, puppy/puffy/putty, steed, bullet, waddle, waffle, soggy, rudder, rubber, rugger

A Horse Vocabulary - page 7.

1. knacker 2. piebald 3. skewbald 4. thrush 5. farrier 6. ostler 7. Shetland 8. bridle, bit 9. sire, dam 10. withers 11. thoroughbred, standardbred 12. bearing rein 13. colt 14. filly 15. hands 16. dog 17. curry 18. teeth 19. loose 20. blinkers 21. break 22. Clydesdale.

Place Where People and Animals Live - page 8.

```
E Y R I F C L D O K E N
S K C E O E L G V M O N
B A A M R M N U E A N E
S R R A C O Y E C S T U
E S S N V N A L O S E R
O U E N E N H B T H L Y
H G V A I T S A E E L P
E N A R G L S T S C O O
V O C A O O E R T R O F
I L A H W S E S U O H K
H E R N E R W O N W E R
L O D G E R A R A M B O
                      W
```

1. stable 2. fortress 3. warren 4. eyrie 5. hive 6. kennel 7. form 8. lodge 9. web 10. shell 11. dovecote 12. coop 13. barracks 14. whare 15. longhouses 16. igloo 17. workhouses 18. caravan 19. monastery 20. manor 21. convent 22. cell 23. gunyah 24. manse.

Words and Expressions from Other Languages - page 9.

```
A R D N O P A U T A T S
M D E X O E N S H C A D
G I Z P V R N Q S H T Z
R A S O O D O U O U I E
A S I P M I N I D N N L
L V L U L I E M T D H A
A O E D E C O A S E C I
M U A U T L D U I S T
O S P L A G O E L G R A
D E M E T N E R R E D N
S U P T E N O T B R H A
F U G I R I N G O A G W
```

1. Mardi Gras 2. tempus fugit 3. schnitzel 4. Notre Dame 5. Erin go Bragh 6. wanderlust 7. eau de Cologne 8. vox populi 9. Anno Domini 10. Dei gratia 11. dachshund 12. á la mode 13. status quo 14. répondez s'il vous plaît Latin was spoken in ancient Rome.

One Word to Describe a Group - page 10.

1. trees 2. diseases 3. snakes 4. newspapers 5. fish
6. meat 7. directions/compass points 8. pop groups/bands
9. footwear 10. football teams 11. guns 12. writers
13. money/currency 14. cricketers 15. spiders
16. companies 17. oceans 18. ships 19. boats 20. religions
21. even numbers 22. cars 23. insects 24. aeroplanes
25. reference books 26. bones 27. horses 28. tools
29. dogs 30. rivers 31. seas 32. jewels 33. metals
34. flowers 35. stone fruits 36. teeth 37. camels
38. deserts 39. golf clubs 40. explorers 41. odd numbers
42. materials 43. goats 44. fast foods 45. flightless birds
46. squares 47. rulers 48. soccer terms 49. flags
50. football 51. artists 52. stars 53. musical instruments
54. disasters 55. Prime Ministers 56. Scottish heroes
57. trains/famous train lines 58. racehorses 59. detectives
60. music notes 61. computers/computer brands 62. salad
vegetables 63. music styles 64. paints 65. ethnic groups/
nationalities/languages.

Animal Families Worksheet - page 12.

Exercise A - 1. classification 2. vertebrates 3. gills
4. cold-blooded 5. water 6. dry, scaly 7. reptiles 8. light,
hollow 9. monotremes 10. insects.
Exercise B - teacher to correct.
Exercise C - 1. smooth, wet 2. it's on the outside
3. internal skeleton, two legs, no thorax, no stages, no wings.

Living Things - page 13.

Fish - 1. shark 2. whiting 3. cod 4. plaice 5. perch
6. bream 7. salmon 8. sole 9. carp 10. trout 11. mullet
12. mackerel 13. tuna 14. stingray 15. flat head 16. marlin
17. haddock 18. barracuda 19. groper 20. pike 21. skate
22. flounder.
Reptiles - 1. asp 2. grass snake 3. dinosaur 4. viper 5. gecko
6. anaconda 7. rattlesnake 8. crocodile 9. adder
10. lizard 11. alligator 12. sidewinder 13. cobra 14. python
15. tortoise 16. chameleon 17. iguana 18. monitor lizard.
Birds - 1. swan 2. swallow 3. turkey 4. albatross 5. goose
6. canary 7. peacock 8. budgerigar 9. kiwi 10. magpie
11. flamingo 12. duck 13. falcon 144. seagull 15. buzzard
16. vulture 17. robin 18. sparrow 19. penguin 20. chicken
21. swift 22. pelican.
Mammals - 1. cat/bat/rat 2. horse 3. whale 4. reindeer
5. fox/dog 6. mouse 7. rabbit 8. elephant 9. ape
10. antelope 11. hyena 12. giraffe 13. beaver 14. zebra
15. gorilla 16. panther 17. goat 18. tiger 19. kangaroo
20. dolphin 21. seal 22. camel.
Insects - 1. moth 2. beetle 3. termite 4. cockroach 5. flea
6. locust 7. earwig 8. mosquito 9. wasp 10. cricket
11. dragonfly 12. honeybee 13. gnat 14. hornet 15. silverfish
16. ladybird 17. louse 18. weevil.
Flowers - 1. rose 2. daisy 3. snowdrop 4. chrysanthemum
5. lily 6. dahlia 7. bluebell 8. carnation 9. pansy 10. orchid
11. begonia 12. lavender 13. poppy 14. violet 15. daffodil
16. sunflower 17. iris 18. tulip.

Science and Technology - page 14.

Space and Space Travel - 1. Earth 2. Pluto 3. astronaut
4. galaxy 5. star 6. Venus 7. Jupiter 8. satellite 9. quasar
10. rocket 11. Neptune 12. universe 13. comet

14. planet 15. asteroid
16. spaceship 17. moon 18. Saturn
19. Mercury 20. meteorite 21. Mars
22. Uranus 23. sunspot 24. constellation.
Elements - 1. sodium 2. silver 3. uranium
4. magnesium 5. iron 6. copper 7. calcium 8. chlorine
9. zinc 10. oxygen 11. sulphur 12. phosphorus 13. gold
14. carbon 15. nitrogen 16. hydrogen 17. lead 18. nickel
19. platinum 20. plutonium.
The Weather - 1. winter 2. summer 3. thunder 4. lightning
5. frost 6. season 7. drought 8. heatwave 9. fog
10. autumn 11. tornado 12. thermometer 13. cloud
14. spring 15. whirlwind 16. temperature 17. rain
18. cyclone 19. blizzard 20. hurricane 21. snow
22. rainbow 23. atmosphere 24. meteorology.
The Plant Kingdom - 1. cactus 2. shoot 3. petal 4. vegetable
5. root 6. moss 7. flower 8. cultivate 9. tree 10. fruit
11. shrub 12. branch 13. stem 14. weed 15. pollen
16. fungus 17. leaf 18. lichen 19. photosynthesis.
The Earth's Surface and Environments - 1. river 2. forest
3. iceberg 4. continent 5. lake 6. lagoon 7. jungle
8. waterfall 9. valley 10. desert 11. glacier 12. mountain
13. island 14. tundra 15. volcano.

Which is Which? - page 15.

1. fingers, toes 2. caterpillars, grubs 3. Australia, Australasia
4. practice, practise 5. apes, monkeys 6. tortoises, turtles
7. Antarctica, Arctic 8. melody, lyrics 9. moths, butterflies
10. hurdle, steeplechase 11. numerals, numbers
12. margarine, butter 13. toads, frogs 14. iron, steel
15. porpoises, dolphins, porpoises, dolphins.

Hidden Animals - page 16.

1. hen 2. cat 3. bull, lion 4. rat 5. ape 6. ass 7. mole 8.
tick 9. crow 10. ox 11. ant 12. bat 13. boar 14. cow, owl
15. crab 16. bear 17. hare 18. fish 19. goat 20. toad 21.
mice 22. frog 23. shark 24. dog 25. flea 26. horse 27.
panther 28. antelope 29. donkey 30. octopus.

Rhyming Words - page 17.

Exercise A - 1. bread and butter 2. steak and kidney
3. baked beans 4. plum pudding 5. custard tart 6. fish and
chips 7. bacon and eggs 8. curry powder 9. fried rice
10. hot dogs with sauce 11. peaches and cream 12. fruit
salad 13. chicken noodle soup 14. pork chops 15. meat
pie 16. milkshake 17. bread and dripping 18. jelly babies
19. roast beef 20. pie and peas.
Exercises B - 1. Tom Thumb 2. Jack Horner 3. Wee Willie
Winkie 4. Bo Peep 5. Mother Goose 6. Little Boy Blue
7. Tom, Tom the Piper's Son 8. Punch and Judy 9. Peter
Piper 10. Miss Muffet. *Extra Question* - Adam and Eve.

Fruit and Vegetables - page 18.

The message reads - Fruit is a very important part of your
diet. fig, grape, cucumber, onion, potato, kiwifruit, swede,
apple, avocado, peach, turnip, blackberry, pineapple, tomato,
parsley, orange, parsnip, lettuce, mandarin, banana,
watermelon, spinach, carrot, raspberry, nut, coconut,
cauliflower, strawberry, olive, satsuma, rhubarb, date,
apricot, leek, brussels sprout.
1. apples 2. potatoes 3. tomatoes 4. cabbages
5. oranges 6. plums 7. pears.

Places and Things - page 19.

1. Mexican 2. Arctic 3. America's 4. French 5. Siamese
6. Indian 7. Indian 8. Chinese 9. Welsh 10. Panama
11. Welsh 12. Swede 13. Danish 14. Turkish 15. German
16. African 17. Roman 18. Portuguese
19. Irish 20. Victoria.
Activity - Chinese Whispers

Classifying - page 20.

1. library 2. watch 3. stethoscope
4. draught 5. horse 6. wig 7. cat
8. chicken 9. sew 10. ring pull tab
11. cancer 12. Hello! 13. lake 14. ice hockey 15. penguin
16. worm 17. ladybird 18. Berlin 19. trousers 20. rose
21. dog 22. circle 23. Robin Hood 24. shin 25. tram
26. typewriter 27. fried egg 28. triangle 29. trumpet
30. python 31. nail 32. starfish 33. £15 34. seed
35. dolphin 36. fraction 37. Michael Jackson 38. diamond
39. pyjamas 40. horse.

Association - page 21.

1. children, pencils 2. vine, seeds 3. century, centimetre
4. bears, porridge 5. bird, extinct 6. manger, Wise Men
7. pyramid, sphinx 8. blades, hovering 9. racquet, ball
10. gorilla, chimp 11. stars, asteriods 12. golden, eyrie
13. stamp, letter 14. mosque, Muslim 15. Greece,
marathon 16. sand, towel 17. tutu, audience 18. tree,
tapper 19. Greenland, igloo 20. web, arachnid 21. metal,
mineral 22. judge, jury 23. stump, Lords 24. Mersey,
Severn 25. cry, tears 26. tiles, thatch 27. animals, flood
28. headline, article 29. leather, heel 30. collar, sleeve
31. scales, gill 32. stem, petals 33. keyboard, cursor
34. lens, rims 35. kimono, origami 36. stable, whinny
37. toe, ankle 38. mast, sails 39. shearer, wool 40. soprano,
compact disc.

Spaghetti Words - page 22.

Terms used in Sport - 1. leg before wicket 2. on your marks
3. hole in one 4. on the boundary 5. putting for par
6. Marylebone Cricket Club 7. backhand passing shot
8. front row forward 9. three-legged race 10. caught and
bowled.
Famous People - 1. Good King Wenceslas 2. Sir Issac
Newton 3. John the Baptist 4. Leonardo da Vinci
5. HG Wells 6. Ludwig Von Beethoven 7. Martin Luther
King 8. Sir Winston Churchill 9. Sheriff of Nottingham
10. Joan of Arc 11. Robert the Bruce 12. Alfred the Great.
Well-known Trios - 1. stiff upper lip 2. here, there and
everywhere 3. Flopsy, Mopsy and Cottontail 4. sugar,
spice and all things nice 5. hook, line and sinker 6. Caspar,
Melchior and Balthazar 7. Huey, Dewey and Louie
8. lock, stock and barrel 9. ear, nose and throat
10. animal, vegetable and mineral.

Choose an Ending - page 23.

1. horse 2. bat 3. cast 4. train
5. cake 6. dance 7. pool 8. nail
9. fly 10. paper 11. side 12. match
13. hat 14. boots 15. coat
16. time 17. chop 18. bag

19. fall 20. ship 21. worm 22. case 23. way 24. bird
25. chair 26. maid 27. star 28. ball 29. sense 30. berry.
Extension - 1. ducks 2. smith 3. cut 4. food 5. radio.

Beginnings and Endings - page 24.

Bird - pelican, Canada *Greedy* - selfish, fisherman
Big Person - giant, antenna *Small house* - cottage, agent
Send overseas - export, porter *Sport* - tennis, island
Leave - depart, partner *Woodland* - forest, restless *In the
open* - outside, sideline *Mend* - repair, aircraft *Not fresh* -
stale, alert *Current* - recent, centurion
Going forever - endless, lesson *Fish* - flounder, understand
Sport - football, ballerina *Vegetable* - carrot, rotate
Bird - sparrow, rowdy *Rider* - cyclist, listen *Business
partnership* - company, anybody *Earth* - planet, netball
Order - command, Andersen *Plant bed* - garden, dentist
To be present - attend, endanger *Error* - mistake, takeaway
Body part - heart, artist *Hut* - cabin, insect.

Starting Words - page 25.

Star Trek - start, starve, starling, starboard, startle, starch
and stargazer.
Cats in the Belfry - catalogue, catapult, Catherine Wheel,
catalyst, caterpillar, cathedral, Catholic, catamaran,
catastrophe and cattle.
Ant Attack - Antarctica, antenna, antelope, anthem,
antiseptic, antidote, Antigua and Antipodes.
Early Man - manacle, manager, mandarin, mango, mandolin,
mannequin, mansion and manufacturer.

Odd One Out - page 26.

1. bee, ant, <u>dry</u>, fly 2. hand, foot, <u>lion</u>, nose
3. brown, black, <u>jelly</u>, green 4. chair, table, stool, <u>drink</u>
5. rugby, <u>mouse</u>, tennis, soccer 6. <u>plastic</u>, coffee, cocoa,
lemonade 7. kitten, puppy, piglet, <u>elbow</u> 8. skirt, blouse,
dress, <u>cement</u> 9. <u>marbles</u>, truck, train, bicycle 10. pelican,
seagull, <u>snoring</u>, stork 11. <u>Italy</u>, piano, trumpet, flute
12. cabbage, <u>sparrow</u>, lettuce, spinach 13. <u>pound</u>, river,
brook, swamp 14. tractor, bulldozer, harvester, <u>thimble</u>
15. butcher, <u>camel</u>, baker, grocer.

Matching Pairs - page 27.

Exercise A - fez, Turkey turban, India sombrero, Mexico
bowler, England beret, France cork hat, Australia.
Exercise B - Jack Tar, sailor Bobby, policeman brickie,
bricklayer ham, actor beak, magistrate
chippie, carpenter.
Exercise C - Numismatist, coins Philatelist, stamps
Discophile, records Phillumenist, matchbox tops
Lepidopterist, butterflies Bibliophile, books.
Exercise D - Black Beauty, horse Andy Pandy, rag doll
Pinocchio, puppet Moby Dick, whale Shere Khan, tiger
Babe, pig.
Exercise E - Edison, light bulb Bell, telephone
Baird, television Marconi, radio Gutenberg, movable type
Galileo, telescope Sikorsky, helicopter Benz, motor car.
Exercise F - electron, atom crust, pie tongue, bell plasma,
blood bronze, copper horn, unicorn.

Answers

Exercise G - kangaroo, Australia llama, Peru mongoose, India yak, Tibet panda, China orang-utan, Borneo.

Exercise H - sumo wrestling, Japan baseball, USA cricket, England polo, Persia/India golf, Scotland hurling, Ireland.

Exercise I - femur, thigh skull, head pelvis, hips radius and ulna, forearm tarsus, ankle metacarpal, wrist.

Exercise J - Napoleon, France Cleopatra, Egypt St Patrick, Ireland Simon Bolivar, Venezuela George Washington, USA Ghandi, India Alfred the Great, England Good King Wenceslas, Czechoslovakia.

Unfamiliar, Familiar Words and Phrases - page 29.

upstairs, hole in one, reading between the lines, one square metre, Her Royal Highness, tricycle, London Bridge, top hat, misunderstanding, slim chance, wolf in sheep's clothing, fast asleep, swarm of bees, underarm deodorant, thirty degrees right.

What's my Number? - page 30.

1. hundreds, thousands 2. ten
3. seven 4. three 5. nine 6. two,
three 7. seven 8. one 9. four 10. ten
11. three 12. twenty-one 13. seven 14. five 15. three
16. two 17. twelve 18. nine 19. four 20. three 21. seventy 22. four 23. seven 24. two 25. three 26. three.

Number Language - page 31.

1. mix 2. crocodile 3. mill 4. limit 5. lid 6. civic 7. dime 8. elixir 9. civil 10. mice 11. vice 12. livid 13. decimal 14. vim 15. mild.

Name-dropping - page 32.

1. brute, nose 2. ferry, tuna 3. bark, mean 4. briar, large 5. bent, lawn 6. dames, Zulu 7. giant, ant 8. baron, Mars 9. dance, sane 10. Rover, penny 11. bully, rat 12. job, leggy 13. navy, pill 14. Hardy, label 15. berry, moan 16. gent, angels 17. waiter, sun 18. warden, jam 19. duke, fancy 20. charges, fat 21. tennis, jelly 22. drank, windy 23. grey, jetty 24. care, began 25. mice, rush 26. plan, bossy 27. free, trace 28. nail, list 29. star, merry 30. tiny, luck 31. core, rim 32. shape, salty 33. kidney, alive 34. tie, icy 35. moss, holly 36. rodeo, panda 37. drug, feather 38. olive, dizzy.

Words in Words - page 33.

Food - peach, pear, bun, veal, rice, egg, cream, pea, pie, corn, ham, oats.

Body - arm, hand, skin, lip, shin, liver, hair, chin, ear, rib, lung, hip.

Boy's Names - Tom, Ted, Scot, Pete, Stan, Ken, Ern, Roy, Alan and Lance, Con, Vince and Ed, Tim, Sid, Ian, Rick, Ron, Len, Mark, Victor.

Girl's Names - Sue, Ruth, Pat, Anne, Tina, Cath, Dora, Lisa, Grace, Monica, Ada, Eve.

Animals - Cat, Rat, Lion, boar, hen, bat, wren, cow/owl, ass, eel, teal, moth, ape, mole.

Words in Words II - page 34.

Answers will vary.

Long and Short Vowels - page 35.

Long Vowels - take, cake, bite, bone, lone, home, white, date, gate, bake, rake, lake, make, wake, cone, phone, kite, tone, state, hate, late, cube, tube, mate, like.

Short Vowels - back, sack, bit, kit, grub, fog, sit, tack, dog, lack, fit, hit, rack, lit, pit, tub, bog, cub, sat, hat, fat, hum, bag, ham.

Syllables - page 36.

Exercise A - 1. spelling 2. handwriting 3. punctuation 4. comprehension 5. mathematics 6. geometry 7. investigations 8. calculations.

Exercise B - 1. Pluto 2. Mercury 3. Jupiter 4. Uranus 5. constellations 6. galaxies 7. asteroid 8. meteor 9. astronauts.

Exercise C - 1. tremendous 2. enormous 3. colossal 4. gigantic 5. astronomical 6. voluminous 7. substantial 8. extensive.

Building Blocks - page 37.

M	R	E	N	S	E	S	E	H	S	H	R
C	R	C	H	O	D	S	E	S	T	S	A
K	I	N	R	O	W	I	R	A	O	C	K
N	M	Y	R	G	G	N	A	H	B	S	I
A	H	I	O	**G**	**O**	I	P	U	R	G	N
R	C	I	R	T	**L**	K	S	N	I	L	L
F	L	A	Y	W	**D**	Y	A	D	R	T	I
B	E	N	R	E	L	B	C	D	E	N	A
A	M	U	A	E	V	A	B	S	P	E	S
L	T	A	N	E	B	A	L	P	I	N	G
I	H	A	A	F	Y	N	A	H	K	I	M
E	S	Z	A	R	T	H	R	E	E	T	Y

1. twelve 2. January 3. Epiphany 4. three kings 5. wise 6, 7 and 8. Caspar, Melchior and Balthazar (in any order) 9. brilliant 10. baby king 11. hundreds 12. gold 13. frankincense 14. myrrh 15. La Befana 16. good 17. stockings 18. ashes

Letters Spell - Merry Christmas.

Multiple Meanings - page 39.

1. light 2. bit 3. ball 4. nut
5. safe 6. orange 7. fly 8. kid
9. run 10. top 11. last
12. march 13. fast
14. iron 15. second.